THE MINISTRY OF FLOWERS

Andrea Witzke Slot is a London-based poet and fiction writer. After teaching for many years (primary school in the UK, then at Collin College in Texas and at the University of Illinois at Chicago after earning her PhD), Andrea now lives in London where she works as a contributing artist with Fiona Lesley's Poetry Exchange and tries to capture the unexpected beauty of humanity and nature in words, paints, piano and photography. Her publications include *To find a new beauty* (Gold Wake Press 2012), a poetry collection inspired by H.D.'s Sea Garden poems.

The Ministry
of Flowers

ANDREA WITZKE SLOT

Valley Press

First published in 2020 by Valley Press
Woodend, The Crescent, Scarborough, YO11 2PW
www.valleypressuk.com

ISBN 978-1-912436-43-9
Cat. no. VP0171

Cover design by Jamie McGarry.
Cover illustration by Andrea Witzke Slot.
Text design by Peter Barnfather.
Edited by Jo Brandon.

Printed and bound in Great Britain by
Imprint Digital, Upton Pyne, Exeter.

Contents

for my various families
whose love and kindness span countries, continents, genres, forms

for Ava, Liam and Hannah who scatter flowers everywhere

and for Peter, always

Between My Country—and the Others—
There is a Sea—
But Flowers—negotiate between us—
As Ministry.

—Emily Dickinson

My religion is very simple. My religion is kindness.

—Dalai Lama

Panoply

Some days the rigid silhouette of all we are is revealed in plates of glass. Some days we might touch the strange mesh of armour that keeps us upright and steady and wonder at how little keeps us from flopping into heaps on the floor like the billowing collapse of a circus tent as stakes are pulled from the ground. And yet, my doctor tells me, we are all disappearing, year by year, tick at a time, even with those bite-sized chalks of calcium, glasses of milk, spoonfuls of yogurt. Nothing can halt the slow exiting of cells as they fade from our axial skeletons: the bones that run up our vertebral columns, the bones that circle our hips and encage our chests, the bones that jut upward to our skulls and outwards to our hands and feet. We are all unrehearsed vanishing acts, a case of self thinning out until, one day, we too are hunched over sidewalks, only able to see our own feet moving in front of us. But this is a gradual farewell, announced over long stretches of time, and is, in fact, cause for great celebration. We are the progenitors of our own destruction and no outside force can stop the dissolution of all that we are, all we inhabit in this moment, as you read these words, touch another's face, or slip away from the town's cool edge. Don't miss the fanfare. Look up and see. All around you, people are slowly waving goodbye.

Between my country and the others—a sea

spreads its glassy surface, a sea smooth
      as robin's-egg-blue. But year by year
(remember when we were young?) shells ground
      vision to winter's beachy grit.
If I cannot see your distant lands,
      blame it on arcs of salt-strewn
mistakes, time's water-logged pastures and roads,
      my sad country of sand-packed pitch.

But do not worry. Florae converse
      as water recedes into earth. See?
Spring arrives. Seedlings sickle upward
      along drying roads, through egg-shell
culture, where (sweet with bees) floret tongues
      point the way to bridge-wide aster-seas.
Love, I'm on my way, flowers in hand. Please
      beg me to come, to travel well.

—after Emily Dickinson (F-40, #905)

The Incubator

Worldworn sleeper, what is tied inside
branches of sapling lungs? Tell me to try
again. To believe in what cannot be seen.
Or touched. That story. Our fingers lean

against your walls of caged glass,
and, inside, mere ounces of flesh
showcase the perfect specimen of
something even stranger than love.

And in what hour of what night was a second
bow pressed to your case, looped around a name
I cannot speak? Who arrived and did I sleep?
No need to tell me, you were born to keep

still as buried faith. Sunbather, go on doing
what you do. Which is to say—do nothing
at all. I'll keep watch as you soak in the sun's rays,
bask in an artificial summer that shines day

and night in your bottled world. Let roots unfold
in a climate of change, as warm as maternal soil.
What dream lies beneath carbon's septic stealth?
Your chest answers with a twitch. A whole self

responds. Don't tell me what could have been
or explain what's wrapped inside oxygen's thin
exchange. Just teach me to expect more—not less—
from this unwrapped bundle of earth, bone, flesh.

Memory is not a peacock landing on a sleeve,

more a wren
  that is

hardly noticeable
  rarely catchable

we have a pot of spaghetti
  boiling on the stove

and the mail has arrived
  and there's a future still to write

but sometimes we
  stop

peer out
  a window

and see a hedgerow
  shuddering

Remember when we thought we'd live forever?

Time dropped slowly on that island
on which we played,

when we'd dive into the surf,
swim in and out of the flesh

we were beginning to own,
sensing the tremor

of volcanic keys rising
beneath our toes,

our soon-to-be cities
buzzing beneath the sea.

We were no one's enemies,
although enemies we knew

for heartbreak, too, was a forever bond
on the island of Forever—

All of it: good and evil—
it would last forever.

All of it: pain and pleasure—
a fate graffitied on the skies above.

We were charmed and we were charming,
and we were doomed by the foreverness of Forever.

Some nights at the back of the Island
makeshift nightclubs pumped oxygen

into our electric bodies and we longed
to share the love we held like sand in our hands

under the midnight suns of Forever.
But remember? Things were hard, too,

in Foreverland. Unforgiving
and devastatingly sad.

And yet it was never easier
than it was then. For Foreverland

was where our souls drank dreams
madly, wildly, deeply.

But tell me—do you remember
the night the boat left the shore?

When the wind took us by the hand?
When we were too busy dancing and crying

to notice? When the party somehow
moved *en masse* from land to ship

and the ship released its anchor
and we were shouting *Forever!* from the helm

as we downed margaritas and saluted
the sunset blooming in the horizon ahead?

And do you remember turning
around to look behind us at dawn?

When we realised where we had been—
and that the Island was gone?

The Time-Being of Oak,
and this too is a political poem

*because in times like these | to have you listen
at all, it's necessary | to talk about trees.*
—Adrienne Rich, 'What Kind of Times are These'

There are Oaks that stand. Oaks that stand forlorn. Oaks in places you notice them. Oaks in places you don't. Oaks that observe cars on roadways. Oaks that guard pathways into towns. Oaks that root themselves deep in the earth of parks and hedges and muddy gardens of childhood homes. Oaks that loom large over supermarket crowds. And surely this too is kindness, a code of ethics, a way of saying, *I am here, and here I will remain.* For how else can we know time-being, time been, the long-ago infancy of acorns and the great blossoming statues of adulthood? How else can we believe that an Oak's ten million offspring will continue to be swept forward in the running rivers after massive, massive rain? How else can we believe in reaching for the wide sky for 100 for 400 for 1000 years? The stratosphere swallows the world into its wet, earthy stomach. Night thunders the spines of all creation. But morning for the Oak always comes. Hear the branches reverberate. See the mud soften like grief beneath our feet. Feel ropes of roots push onward and outward, ripping through steel pipes, cracking foundations, tearing up roads and pavements and fields sown with aversion and hate. And yet there are those who underestimate the dangerous clout of trees. Those who disregard the warnings of birdsong. Those who set up homes and even telephone wires right under the extraordinary shade of so many ordinary, everyday trees.

The Slug

*'It is unlikely that our ancestors ever had to
avoid packs of predatory slugs or snails.'*
—Graham Davey

Sitting damp
as a limp *casarecce*
lump, as heavy
as a drop of play-
dough, you are
never in a hurry,
rain-thirsty drop
of slime, plucked
as you are from
my lettuce leaves.
I never meant
to put you in danger
as I lowered you
to the rain-
slick sidewalk,
but how you pleaded
little more than
slow competence
as you set off
on your cool steady
slide, never once
bracing yourself
for the bang
of a wooden gate,
the gush of
rainy-day laughter,
much less
the murderous
thump of eight

muddy boots
as four children
dashed along
the path,
splashed toward
an open door
where they
yelled *Safe!*
and pulled
themselves
backwards
into a roof-
covered shell
called home—
and so
with my toe
I nudged you
to the dirt
for your
inauspicious
but heartfelt
funeral
lifted a spadeful
of sludge onto
your flat back
and I sat
on the sidewalk
in that pouring rain
and said an elegy
for you, some-
how knowing
my lettuces
would grow

strong
and wide
in the spring
waters of
all you gave
(and didn't take)
in the muddled
compost of
predator/prey
kindness/fate.

Letters from Abroad

My Country
sits alone on a hill even
when the population grows.
My Country sits alone on a hill
and looks out at the mountains.
My Country is quite often a mess
of memory and longing
and skin makes for
a strange strange fence.
My Country has been hurt
and caused hurt
and for this I am
very sorry.
Sometimes I take
my boat from the dock
and set sail across the river.
I yell over the water and up
to the many-splendoured stars
I LOVE YOU.
And sometimes I hear
I LOVE YOU
calling back calling back
calling falling
light as grace
on a cold winter's night
like ashes
from a camp
many miles hence
where another
Country warms
her hands
by a fire
and stares up at

the halo of stars
we've both
come to
see—

Lessons from the Queen of the Lasius Niger

Witness the birth of a nation,
a billion tiny lives, a trillion elfin daughters
who spin themselves into silken cocoons,
domed balls of energy that thrive
on their mother's spit and piss
for there is, by god, little else to take.
Do not be fooled: colonies of sisters will emerge
with the power to build a new world—
eyeless creatures who will morph into beautiful young adults,
scarlet soldiers who will move to the heartbeat
of their all-knowing Queen. After all,
all blood leads to her, their single mother,
who left their father, now dead, on her nuptial flight.
And for a few days their mother was so alone,
never to be that alone again. Did she know
what she was doing when she shimmied off
her wings and disappeared into the dirt?
Did she know that from her trauma
an empire would rise, a nation fuelled
by hard labour and armies of feminist might?

Blood Ties, circa 1932

for my grandmother

Do you know her? The woman
who pulled heirloom tomatoes

from the twisted vines
of her garden?

Who staked, twined,
pruned and watered daily?

I know a few things.
I know that each evening she'd wait

for her first husband (a minister
who knew the reddened shame

of humanity) to come
home to dinner.

I know she diced,
sliced, chunked, pressed

the fruity flesh into sauce,
tossed its meat into meals

that kept bellies warm
in the crossed circuits

of veins, in the closed
fists of hearts.

And I know her husband
grew tired of living in boxes,

even boxes with doors,
boxes with windows

like the one in which you now sit
as you stare out

into the grey street
at the grey homes,

at the orange-handled ladder
that rests against the house opposite.

So much I don't know.
So much I want to ask.

Such as: Why did he squeeze
the tomatoes in his hand,

issue of seed and bee and soil,
and watch the juice crawl between his fingers?

And why that Sunday
after his sermon—before dinner—

did he step into the garage,
settle himself behind the wheel of his car

(as if preparing for an evening
drive) and turn on the engine?

And I want to know: how did
this woman's tomatoes feel

in her hand as she pulled the orbed
offspring from autumn's coiling vines

and went on to give birth
to the noisy boy called my father.

And most of all: did she forget?
Or did life become daily witness

to a thousand unmade meals:
all she found undone

in the garage that next morning
the achene preparation

the plate that sat
on the oak table for days?

What recovery looks like

Do you know the girl who smiles
in the photographs on my bookshelves?
Have you seen her?
The one who got up like a shadow
and dove into faded images
taken by no one?

The clouds are only smoke,
she said, as she pulled her hand through
the grey haze.

Only smoke, I said, as my hand followed hers.

Only smoke, she said. Like memories.
Like time courses through a body,
releases its poison, its lure,
its here and now, where roils
of ineptitude take the heat, swallow the fire.

It can't be held, I said.

It's the over, she answered. The vanished.
The breathing that's done from the future
when all you know steps into the ocean,
dissolves in the waters of what once was.

Will you return? I asked.

Yes, she said. Re-
assembled. Like mist.

Can something reassemble
once particles dissolve? I asked.
Can something rewind, step backwards
onto waves?

I see the avocets, she said.
I see relearning. How hard
can it be to stand on sand?

The Psychologists' Room

has been empty of psychologists for years now, but still their sound-proofed siding squirrels through the walls added to our home long before we arrived with our children, our dog, our noise. As if what is said in this room, stays in this room. They arrange their chairs around my scratched wooden desk, shuffle toward me, saying *just relax, get comfortable, yes, put your feet up,* and then begin with small talk that quickly tumbles into large talk. Daily I interrupt them, the soft weeping, their handed-over Kleenex reaches, the tell-me-more of their stares; I spin my chair away from them, put down my book, and retreat to the kitchen. Mere minutes pass before I return, hesitating as I push open the door, momentarily sure that they are the no-longer, echoes of what's left behind. They know better. And so I settle at my desk, and there, with my head bent, my fingers in motion, I submit to their queries and cross-examinations, letting them analyse my absent voice, all I never did, all I did too well, pulling sorry from my lungs where always it sits, always it burns, and this room is not just a room but you and me and the gods of everything taking notes, and these words are so damned quiet that I can't even hear the dog outside the door barking to come in, barking.

Last Day to Save on Sarah Jaeger's 'Throwing and Alternative Video'

—*Ceramics Monthly* advertisement

No longer interested in *why*,
    sign me up for the master class
      of *how*.

Train me to be an able student, Sarah.
      Teach me the art of kneading mud,
cupping slabs, spinning and shaping
    lumps of cool,
        wet earth.
      Let me be your apprentice,
        your tyro intern—

    How I long to dip my hands
        into spinning vats,
still the world into objects of practical design.

But *alternatives*, Sarah?
    Just what are the other ways of throwing, moulding,
        fixing,
firing? Please divulge your secrets.
    Please tell all. This is a new call
from one desperate for new
    techniques,
          one who burns
        to learn new tricks
    for solving fire-hardened
      mysteries
of muck,
    mortar, ovens,
bricks.

Please reply soon.
　　　　I have one day left.
　　And my fingers
are hot
　　　　with clay.

Regret

I am sorry I didn't return your call
or answer your second call, or return
your text or email or Facebook message.
It is hard to hear when I am turning, turning,
pulling down computer-lidded eyes, packing up,
walking away. Do you know I wake in the night
thinking of you—yes, thinking of you—wondering
why I didn't return your call, or answer your second call
or kept my phone on silent for days and then weeks
or why I didn't type a response while the computer-
lidded eyes remained propped open toothpick style
for so very long? Don't get me wrong. I love you.
And I have tried to hear you ring and ring and ring
in the way phones used to ring when we were children,
when we all jumped up and ran a mad-dashed race toward
the large yellow-belled instrument, wanting to know
who it was and my sister would win and she would
answer breathlessly and sigh as she surrendered
the plastic dogbone to me, and then you and I would talk
for hours as I leaned against that bright orange kitchen wall
with my fingers sweating and wrapped tight around
the heavy receiver, and I miss you, how I miss you,
even more so since the empty message voice turned up,
stopping your clear rings in their tracks in the way
I wish it could stop all that is now turning, turning,
pulling down, packing up, walking away—

Gemütlichkeit

Take from me this dove's-egg nest
in which you can place your charms
and maybe even a dream
or two. And here. Go on. Take
this cup of mud and feathers,
a nest woven just for you.
Will you put all you carry
in its shelter? Settle close
as I ease you like a song?
Oh, I know pulsating need.
My wings, they are waiting-warm.
But these, my legs? Brittle-cold.
Naked as winter. The sun
draws low, as if it too asks—
Darling, let's undress and rest,
make love on a bed from which
a hundred-year-old trunk grows.
Let's spend the afternoon there,
consent to mischief and sin.
It's quite easy. Just forgive.
And when dark arrives, and death
glows like light in open palms,
may what we earned in cool night's
air, all we learned and all we
shared, find its way from bone to
wing when flesh no longer cares.

Llama: lama glama

*'Llamas are willing pack animals but only to a point.
An overloaded llama will simply refuse to move.
These animals often lie down on the ground and
they may spit, hiss, or even kick at their owners
until their burden is lessened.'*
—*National Geographic*

Flat-headed not-quite-
camel-of-a-beast,
with your frog eyes
sitting up high,
why do you stare
at me tête-à-tête,
with your watery,
floating, ostrich neck?
You are one giant
thumb-like projection,
a chest-swallowed head
that marries your insect legs
in one fell swoop—
and still all that powder puff
fluff of puffer-fish pride.
People think:
How can you be so vain?
How can you be so sure?
Who made you think
you own the place?
I know better.
You were not born knowing
that queenship is your fate.
You are so much more
than a rope or rug, pack-
hauler or pile of dung
(handy as it is for fires).

You are the shyness
no one can see,
the awkwardness
no one realises.
I know the feeling—
refusing to move if
a burden is too heavy,
spitting if you feel
you've been wronged,
hissing if never allowed
to hum your strange tunes
much less take
a moment's rest.
Llama, dear llama,
teach me to wear my eyes
on top of my head,
wear the spit in my mouth,
lift a little pride
onto my brittle back,
and learn how to give,
even in death,
a little something
of use.

Forgetting this problem of dirt and dust

Do you know the days? When the life-dirt wars
become so thick you have no choice but clean?
When, at first light, you find yourself on your knees,
sweeping out cobwebs, dumping out drawers,
wiping smeared windows, washing down floors?

How do you make a home fresh as a new-born?
Undo all that is tarnished? Cure a blood-
bank with brushes and rags, the modest tools
of trust? What hides in the beauty of driven
perdition, in all that's been soiled and riven?

Maybe these rooms beg you to forget spores
of dust. Maybe it's time to forgive the mess
of what's past and stroll outdoors to a place
where chaos meets chance. Love's debris: italics
of seed. Praise bedlam fields. Rest in wild calyces.

Ode to the Stairs

Rectangular boatplanks plopped, nestled and nailed by builders decades dead, foot-perpendicular-by-foot-perpendicular, like the staves of the somewhere-coffins of the three families that once moved up and down these same dropped beams of oak — families I never knew — children I never held — their echoed calls transposed into a music I cannot discern. Once my father and I spent an entire weekend moving in and out and under our home, trying to quell the noise that lived inside our days — the mice-like voices that breathed beneath our heavy feet. It worked. Mostly. But some nights I find myself plodding up and down the routes of what refuses to be silenced — finding in life's reprises the diminutive effort — the slight sips of self we leave behind — and in the dark of 2am, as I climb the stairs with a child in my arms, I find myself stepping home — just a place where being human means but one shared body and one pair of borrowed hands, holding one borrowed child, and then another, and then another, treading on the whiskered trace of all who came before — the same ghost-mount of life's routines — the climbing up — the clambering down — the sleeping — the waking — the worry — so much worry — reduced to a mere whisper that treads into dawn — the inexplicable longing that remains when we are no longer a body or hands or mothers or daughters or fathers or sons — when we too are but under-home notes released beneath slippered feet — squeaking beams of daylight that love and even the most resolute labours will never erase —

Standing near my father's work

Back home, in low evening's light, a window
frames my father's workspace. Outside, a pier
reaches out to coastal currents, shallow

currents that draw near, nearer to him, nearer
to me, as we lean beside a half-painted
canvas in an alcove arranged and cleared

for this untimed work—a room of his own
paid for with labour that kept a family dressed,
fed, sheltered—decades of clocks obeyed.

But that is the past. At his painter's desk,
greying, more eye-to-eye, he speaks of colours
mixed, his latest sketches and brushstroke shifts,

the advice and reviews of his teacher.
I touch a serrated edge where sea meets shore
then sky—and his translation—as my mother

calls to us again and again. We ignore
her even as her familiar song reminds
us of household needs, our daily chores.

But dinner awaits, and I cannot find
the words for all I want to say. I lack
the skills he's mastered. He's found new fire

in a quieter life, ignores ticking clocks
to claim this windowed space for hard-earned tasks—
of talking, painting, and slow beachside walks.

How do we know it's time? I quietly ask.
He answers, *It's always time. Time to rail*
against the rage of engines, time to tack

the waning hours, reach for the furled sails,
hoist them skyward. Time to belay, relax
your grip, release hand over hand. But I fail.

I shade my eyes and watch, putting my trust
in evening's coming winds, the coming-home
work of my father, his canvas, this brush.

Self-portrait, Desk

Elephant-ear patterns of holding,
of keeping upright, of fires not yet lit,
of not using perfectly good legs
to move into places I don't want to go,
or can't go, am too terrified to go.
I am foothold to reams of undone business.
I hear the piano upstairs and wonder
how wood can make such a noise.
Me—I stand silent. Waiting.
Waiting for the movement of pens
to mark my surface, telling me
that timber was not felled in vain,
that hatchets had a right to hollow and gut,
that boats had a right to pull trees down rivers,
that those rivers were not disappointed
or dog-tired by the act, that they didn't deliver
murdered but resurrected copses,
reformed corpses, shaped into useful boxes
for itemised bills and unwritten memoirs,
lists of household chores, fragments
of stories, and unfinished poems.
And so it is: me, as still and quiet
as a secret drawer, and sometimes
I feel the heat of a scorching
summer's drought, and I am reminded
that I am. I am here. And here I will remain.
As steadfast as my maker's initials carved deep
in my chest. And what am I waiting for,
I hear you ask? Pull up a chair. Yes—
what exactly?

The Palm of Proprioception

The sense of touch arrives early, long before the others, coiling inside our tiny selves as we lie swaddled in the cottony comfort of pre-memory and fishtailed time. And so it will remain until the bitter end, clinging to our skin long after eyesight and hearing fades, long after the taste of food dulls, long after the scent of a loved one's clothes wheedles away into the particled air. Rest assured, it will haunt us even in our final hours, as the cool night air floats into our empty rooms to shroud our failing lives. Touch, you see, is not just about love, consolation, sex or need. Touch is the heat of others pulling at the spine-needled compass within, telling us who we are, where we are, and when. *Direction* is the meat of this unassailable craving, sewn into every thousandth millimetre of us from the instant we are plunged into the cold air of the world, held up in a doctor's hand, placed near another's body, our naked skin lit—if we are lucky—by the light-like pulse of another. You know the stories: infants whose lungs shut down from lack of touch, who die lying in their false-sun incubators, barred from the grief of those who press their fingers against walls of glass. How many of us hunger for what others take for granted? A brush of a hand in ours as we cross a street? The heat of an embrace as we exit a train? A pair of legs intertwined with ours in the night? A body on ours in an open-wide dawn? When touch doesn't arrive, radars fail. Vessels drift into Bermuda triangles where there is no longer an *under*, a *back*, a *down*. But even then—when magnetic fields scramble sense—the dream of direction continues: reveries of bodies floating in the salty balm of island-calm waters, where every inch of flesh is warmed, every organ gloved, where our whole selves are cradled in the boats of furnaced hands, rocking, rocking, rocking.

Inscriptions

You—dictionary—say there is no word
inscripted, but I know your pages lie.
I know my child's existence is furled
not on but *in* my flesh: scrolled designs plied
on the pockmarked skin of mother-love.
Look closely. See the words of needled tattoos
snake through muscled veins of daughter-love,
her voice encrypted in bone. Oh, I know inscripted.
I know patterns of night-fired furnaces—
when my daughter would disappear for days, riddled
by legions of need. Years passed. She returned.
Did you know *courage* means *joy* when stitched in scars?
So tell me—how can your pages claim truth
when I open a body inscripted with proof?

Geometric

Meet my geometric shapes
puzzled into others,
a princess of Picasso regret,
a cheek that meets north,
a chin that leaves west,
just segments of self
angled in reflex movement—
not blurred—but pencilled
with precision and hard-
bitten lines and if I
can't see from but one side
of one cheek, from but one eye,
if I no longer understand
what you ask of me, please try
to forgive my scissored flaws
the way one might forgive
Picasso or anyone who has the skill
to fracture a body a head an eye
and still make sense of
a wild hammer and the acute
cost of breaking hearts.

The Daffodils

I'd been a new mother for a little while,
a new friend visit she said with a smile—
we chatted over tea and cake as babies cried.
Cup in hand, she strolled to the window and sighed.
She gazed at the daffodils swaying in the garden
—daffodils that would hearten any heart.
Can I take a few? she turned to ask.
Who am I to say no? *I'll help with the task.*
Every snip, snip, snip, was a blow blow blow,
until there were few daffodils left to know.
She finished her tea, left with a laugh, her hands
full of my happiness. And even now I can't
tell you why it hurt so much—
how in friendship, she stole my trust.

The Suicide Note that Never Was, Note 53

What if tomorrow, as you started your day,
you learned of a suicide note never sent?
Would you begin to rethink all you said and didn't say
as you pull yourself from bed, wash your face and go downstairs?
Would it make you strain to recall all you did and did too well
as you put away the breakfast dishes? Would it make you sigh
as you sit in a chair and stare out the window
at the trees that oxygenate this strangely robust world?
And when you rise from that chair as the afternoon radiators
tick to life, and step into the kitchen to make a cup of tea,
would you find yourself wondering what shards of glass might
feel like when shaped into a boulder? What it might take
to shoulder a misshapen boulder through the blinding rains of need?
As you pour boiling water over the soft tea leaves,
would you move your eyes upward with the rising steam
and squint at the vision that floats in front of you,
the image of a one-person boat awash in the Channel?
Would you wipe tears from your eyes as you return to your chair,
wrap both hands around the heat of your cup,
envisioning the nightsweat dream—the swift
and sudden accident, the unburied pulled down and down?
And in the deep cushion of that chair, with the singe
of tea at your throat, would you wonder at how fate
intervened? How, say, on an autumn night this person
met another person, and began to believe surviving at sea
might be possible? And when the rain begins to hit the window
in the darkening hours, would you sense something ticking to life
inside, as warm as the radiator at your knee? A sense of relief perhaps?
Relief that this person picked up the oars with blood-stained knuckles
and found a way to shore? Would you shake your head a little
as you move to the edge of your chair as night pulls itself
like a blanket over your lawn, especially if you learned
that even now, years hence, this person still prays for you,

you who would have been left behind had that note been sent?
And in bed that night would you feel a burden lighten as you
sense the past collide with the future: how this person wakes
to the daily crash of morning, dips a toe in its cool foamy surf,
and some days even leaps in headfirst to swim beyond
the breakers to float, face up, in the bluer waves
of something pretty damned close to happy?
Would you understand the torn-up note?
Would you learn to forgive?

Out of the Quiet Woods of Marrow and Bone

Our cardiovascular system is a closed system, doctors say, meaning our blood moves down sealed waterways of arteries, veins and capillaries. But the cells that make up the bloodstream were not always part of our body's moving rivers. In fact, they were born in a place as still and quiet as the woods at night—deep inside the soft, spongy marrow of cradled stone. Some of these mushroom-like blasts are homebodies, staying put to mature in the comfort of garden gnomes, while others are quite the adventurers, travelling long distances to remote regions of our bodies' countries where they grow through their adolescent angst. Either way, billions turn into adults that find a way to slip into the flowing rivers of our being. It is there, in these rivers, that we find those cells destined to be leukocytes, tiny angels that quietly fight the good fight, and, even on an ordinary day, tirelessly sieve the rivers of the debris we don't want and, more importantly, don't need. But it is always possible that these rivers might find themselves filled with too much of a good thing, suddenly crowded with all-too-caring cells, damming the rivers in the night. It is then the doctors start calling the result wayward, unfortunate, terminal.

Spindles, Time, Cancer

'It shall not be her death.'
—The Grimms, 'Little Brier-Rose'

Briar no longer grows here, but the spindle
has done its work. One prick, and spiralled springs
unwind themselves as if a magnet sickled
the back of this life-watch, freezing clockwork rigs
that stop but shudder, a tremored pulse
without movement, an echo that parodies
skin and bones. The cogs no longer want wheels,
the rhythmic rush of forward, forward, forward.
Time's rapid continuum falls away,
all moments protracted, set aside, stored.
We are left to stand at her glass case, waiting—
adults telling tales that repeat and reform.
But we too are children. We beg for a fabled release.
Please tell us another story. That she is sound asleep.

—For Rose

Disguises

for Michelle

The scar-line smile
of a crescent moon
on a new year's night.
The empty wine bottles
that line a kitchen counter,
music blaring in the hall.
A wig woven from
the hair of live women.
At a quarter past midnight,
in your absence, we talk,
and, sometimes, we laugh.

Lymphatic

: from Greek numpholēptos 'seized by nymphs'
—Oxford Dictionaries

Snailed inside the riverbanks of our circulatory systems, just under our skin, sleeps a network of tiny nymphs who carry clear running streams of vision. The lungs, gut, and dermis are seasoned by these nymphs, who, at night, gambol along our brooks and becks, along our rivers and lakes. They live not in the cool woods, though. They live in a rain forest, sweaty and fierce with rising heat. Plasma drips everywhere in this land, dribbling from the capillary branches into the worrying roots of our bodies, soaking the very land on which we respire. *Do not fear*, the doctors say in a language I struggle to understand as I stand at my aunt's bedside. *The water-like-goddess-like nymphs are gathering even in the murkiest weather to sing in the soft nodes of her meat, dance on the beans rooted deep in the fleshy earth of her neck, armpits, groin, abdomen, chest.* The nurse adds more words that do not sound like words, sighing, *lean close and you will hear them at night, sieving the poisons, defending the land.* And so I sleep in a chair in a darkened room with red blinking lights and low murmuring sounds as my aunt sleeps for hours and then for days, and sometimes I think I hear them, these elfin-like nymphs, throwing open her gates in the deepest part of dreamtime, swarming the disease-soaked spaces with valiant design and bold delight. I believe. I believe. I believe. They *do* work as they play, providing all the life support they can muster even as they drown in heroic failure. Morning arrives, only to wake to the same steady beats, the same soft breath, the same exhaling seizure of quiet, diabetic slumber.

Appellations

Burnt Oak, London, 1996

I cannot remember her name. But I know she was seven,
that she lived in a half-way house for released prisoners,
a place where the front door had been boarded up long ago,

where people slept on mattresses without sheets, where
there were too few dishes, too little food, too much competition
for everyday needs, for the one toilet, for the three cups

from which all were expected to drink. And yet I know
some things were abundant, copious, viral, silent.
I know she slept under the only entrance into this house:

a window through which men came and went in the nights.
I know rumours of meth, rumours no one could prove,
not the social workers who peered into the streets, her windows,

her eyes. Not the teachers who went to bed, our warm beds,
sick at night. Oh, we could prove what the now-free men once did,
but that was of no consequence—as bonds had been paid,

prison doors unlocked. And I know she slept under that window
in the dank dark, and felt their feet step over her head,
their breath stinking, their clothes rank, their needs sharpened.

The rest I cannot confirm. But I know. I know sometimes
one would bend down to her, drawing her near, touching
her in the way he had longed to touch a girl during

those long years locked inside the metal corridors
of Belmarsh, Wormwood Scrubs, Latchmere:
places with names that sound of leeches,

of lives that don't count, names not remembered. Names
recorded. Names erased. And he was lonely, disgustingly lonely,
and he knew no one would ever know him, know this,

or care. And so she lay there, knowing this man wouldn't
say her name, didn't know her name, didn't care, knowing
she would be back in school in a few hours, her hair in her eyes,

her attempt to hide, to fade from light, wanting no one to see,
to search, to know. And soon she stopped talking altogether,
withdrew from questions, retreated into an imaginary world,

one in which a playground surely still exists,
one in which friends shout her name from across the street,
one in which parents call her home to dinner

with an affectionate, *Now, Pumpkin, please*, and, after
a bath and a favourite book, she is put to bed with a kiss,
a simple kiss, her name whispered as she's tucked under covers,

her small face lit by the pencilled glow of a nightlight,
My little love murmured inside the lullaby of *Goodnight*.

The Unreliable Patient

is an impetuous mess, such unacknowledged need—no wonder no one can look after her. Never taking rest, coughing on others, leaving her blisters to fester longer than necessary, and worse, turn your head for a moment, and she'll sit straight up in her hospital bed, rip the needle from her arm, let the catheter rattle to the floor. You can try to keep an eye on her, but treatments never win. She'll shimmy to the edge of that high bed, jump the long path down, her bare feet smacking a cold white floor. The only thing that's sure is that she'll execute escape. She'll plan her flight like a spy, slip through the bars of casts and wraps, and, with her back to the wall, she'll steal toward the door, where she'll glance up and down the hallway, and when the nurses pass (who'll be looking at their trolleys, syringes in hand), she'll glide out and away, tearing down windowless corridors, her ghost-gown flying behind her, never looking back as the double doors slide open at once, as if they'd been waiting all day for her, as if they were footmen ready to greet her with the smiling signs of emergencies in reverse, and she'll soon slow to a walk, exit red-carpet style, maybe even tousle her hair a little as she leaves behind the fumes of medicine and urine and doctors' orders, and she'll float into the open sunlight and it will be snowing and the sun will be glowing just around the corner of the long street and it will be cold and crisp and it will be so damned bright with all the sickness trapped on the other side of those doors of scrub-room prescriptions and riddled cubes of order, and from the hospital window you'll be helpless—you'll have no choice but to watch her stroll away, for that's all you can do, and you'll sit with your head in your hands, your skull pressed hard against that glass impediment, and you'll watch her shimmer past the squinting corner of those streets and into those distant fields, and soon all you will know is the dot of her rebellion, the paling mark of her body skipping into the green, green forests of all that lies beyond.

Addiction: a definition

The church
           of *need*
       translated
       into bend-
               your-
       self-
               over-
backwards
                       do-
       whatever-it-
takes-
       gotta-have-it-
at-
           any-
       cost
                       now.

       Not recognisable.

So obvious
       that people
       laugh nervously
               in their choice
       to ignore.

Help is
           essential
       to keep it alive
                   and well.

           (Kind people
       think help
                   is
       kindness.)

Hear it? The whirr
    of helicopter blades
        above your home?

Smell it? The blistering
            stench
rising in the evening air
            above
    your neighbourhood?

            Feel it?
        The swirling dirt biting at your
            ankles?

    You might find it
in a stranger's bed
            in the city streets
                                    the gym
                    the pub
            the club
                    a small tidy room where a computer
                                            glows

                    the boarded-up building where
        the needles
            lie.

You know how termites are:
    they silently destroy
            the foundation
    of everything you are.

Pretend you
    don't hear them at night
        the soft chewing on floorboards
    the creak of the wood
beneath your feet
    as you wander the house
        in the dark.

An autobiography called skin

Small, red, rinsed, held. Fleshy folds in tiny fists shaken.
Something like blessings dress the pleats of infant skin.

In shared baths, three sisters inspect split knees and stitched chins.
Laughter mixes with broken words, broken hearts, broken skin.

Long drives of teenage discovery, of mouths, hands, lights dimmed.
Collisions called education, drunken summer nights, near a cool lake, skin to skin.

The *arguer* refuses the *status quo*, works on factory floors, learns *her* bruises are from *him*.
Dialogues sharpen visions of change. Three women swear to defend one another's skin.

And still she exists: the college-girl hubris, the shame of stringbean limbs.
All that can never be. Why can't youth love the smooth deceit of skin?

Mismatched desire in a place I cannot begin or end.
I fall for a man who falls for me. He becomes my country of world-weary skin.

Meet the graduate, love in an upturned bed, a country without kin.
Slough off the old, smile through brutal truths, dress in a pretty wife-skin.

Moments too soon, a firstborn splendour slips into being.
This wide-eyed girl rests *holy* at my breast, feeds from aureole moon-skin.

Years pass: teaching, reading, painting strange synesthetic dreams.
What is love but trying, staying, fighting for what lives inside children's skin?

Bruises yellow in waters of need, as into the world, a second swims.
She unfolds maps to places I've never been, riverscapes of maternal skin.

Courage grows for *them*. Husband turns into *gone*. Back to a country where once I lived.
For two daughters, I learn *alone*: the touch of one between sheets of untouched skin.

Poverty arrives. Two daughters, three jobs, a land-locked PhD. I learn what addiction is.
For nights I cry on a bathroom floor. Prayer lives in many skins.

Dreams die and resurrect. Time grows tired of what we want and intend. We are not the dreams we own. They grow and regrow like this organ called skin.

Redemption arrives on a late autumn night. His voice familiar. Hands warm as sin. Do we merely imagine this hunger for touch, for skin on skin?

Not imagined. Unlatch windows. Throw sashes up. Let love win. See the mark of time passing on open-palmed skin.

A hand rests on my back in the night as trees shiver in autumn's wind. *We are all seasons, dear Andrea. Just rings of skin upon skin upon skin.*

Just another breast poem

for the woman who holds
the two small cushions between

her nimble fingers,
who presses and twists

them into firm positions
against cold glass,

this technician who studies them
in a way no one else does—

one at a time
through her fingers—

and then through the magnified lens
of a camera's widened eyes.

Yes, this is just another breast poem,
though it might not seem one to you.

Here is a plum. Here is another.
The humming heartsong of many lovers

and the ancient river in which
long-ago infants hungrily swam.

Do not worry. If we bathe
with parasites, they will be fished

out with small hooks and poles,
their thin gasping bodies flopping

on a vessel that nets grief.
But only if this woman relieves

me of modesty, this woman
who never wants to find

what daily she seeks—
and as I button

my blouse, ready
to part from her,

she looks at me sadly,
same time, same place?

I watch her small hands,
adjust my bra, and nod.

At a Truck Stop on Highway 124

The odour of stale hotdogs coils
around this truck stop of quiet men
who sit with faces bowed, bath kits
in laps, fair-like tickets in hand.

We take turns flipping through pages
of four-year-old *Time* magazines,
setting one down, picking up another,
sharing the sensation one has when

returning to land after days on a ship,
the road still gravelling beneath our feet,
the car radio still humming in our ears,
the speed unnoticed, natural, easy.

Beyond my rocking body, outside
the window, my hobbled car is hunched
in front of their monster-sized trucks.
Diesel fumes rise in the August heat.

I am not here to rest or shower.
Only to wait for a tow truck driver
who says he'll be here as soon as he can
as an intercom plays its announcement—

steady, monotonous, in a voice
tired of repeating itself:
Shower # _____ *is now available.*
Please proceed to shower # _____.

The men look at their tickets
with mild interest. One stands
and disappears behind a rusty door.
We finger yesterday's news,

and all afternoon the recording repeats—
Shower # _____ is now available.
Please proceed to shower # _____.
And all afternoon, men vanish

and reappear at intervals, with glowing faces
and freshly-combed hair, patches
of clothing clinging to moist chests.
Each slowly exits the room, nodding,

then turns to amble across the cement plains,
the low Texas sun lighting a lowered head.
Cab doors slam shut as each concedes
to transient space, a state of temporary rest,

and I envy them as I lie alone in a dank hotel
that night, longing to pull into tomorrow
alongside them, in a home that is momentary,
moveable, here, and then gone—

Root Position

Life-film of black and white
    in minor keys. There lies
the augmented self. A reaching
    not forward—but back,

down, in. Where notes
    once slid freely to major,
were unchained in C,
    the composition rooted

in Sunday afternoons,
    children's silhouettes
outside panes
    of leaded glass,

two adults sitting
    at an oak table,
newspapers spread,
    agrément of tapping

as a girl's feet pressed pedals,
    released sounds held
for longer than designed,
    sounds like moths

brushing the vibrating chords,
    as if wanting to join
the diminished triads,
    the double sharp arpeggios—

notes heard in different
    ways by different ears,
altered by the unreachable
    pinblock bridge of time

and still this longing—
    to hold the fermata,
to slow this shutting
    of eyes, lips, ears, lids—

The bedroom is where we store the junk of our lives

*'Where can you find a place to keep her, with all the huge strange
thoughts inside you going and coming and often staying all night?'*
—Rilke, *The First Duino Elegy*

On the sentinel called a side table, a blinking eye sits: a glass
of water that watches through the night, lit then not lit then lit
by the tick of the clock, neon ticks tuck tucking you under cool
sheets. And as you stare up at the starless sky, you are never
surprised when the gurgling begins—the stream of water that
runs under your door and spreads itself along the carpet,
swishing up and up and up until it reaches the height of your
bed, until it swallows your feet, your shoulders, your heart, your
head. Nor are you surprised when a thousand tiny hands begin
to lift your mattress, unhooking you from the daytime dock,
launching you off and outward into the dark. As you become
one with the slipstream movement, you peer over the side of
your bed and see yourself being swept from shore, conceding
you have no choice: you must let go all hope for a sandy floor
much less lifeboats or oars. The walls say, *just relax, close your
eyes,* but you whisper, *too late,* for your vision has already
adjusted to the thinning dark, to the current of lost hours, to
the customary as well as the unexpected regrets, the spit-up
relics of shipwrecks that pull sharply through the waves to bob
near—conversations never had, conversations had too often,
children calling for help, mothers calling you home, lovers
calling you to bed, and, and, and, and still the eye continues to
blink in the night, your watchtower, your lighthouse, guiding
you back to the far-away island of morning, watching you with
telescoped vision and tireless time, and then you know it to be
true—there will never be a place to keep her, here with all the
strange thoughts inside you going and coming and staying all
night, here in this midnight ocean in this midnight bed, until—
finally—just as sleep promises to arrive like a rescue boat
bobbing near,

you see
      at the window—
          morning's light
  reaching through the blinds
        like a
          hand,
             outstretched—

Today, after three years of dormancy—

i
- my cactus -
- reminds me -
- it too is alive -
- its capped head -
- lengthening into -
- a poised finger -
- that points -
- the way -
- to the -
- sun -

i

The new bed

I have lain awake in fear:
sure she would roll over,
sure she would forget.
But only a drowsy cry
shakes me from my bed:
a temporary need.

In her cube of darkness,
I stand and listen
to the rhythm of her softly
rising falling chest.
I breathe the air she breathes
conceding I am but witness.

Her star-shaped little-girl figure
becomes progressively clear:
her valiant attempt
to fill the bed's expanse
defeated (tonight)
by the enormity of the charge.
Sentinel of disassembled crib
keeps astute vigil:
dolls, toys, blanket, lie released.
I too release
        —and then draw fingers in tight.

Yet I know I must make
provision for conduit.
I know I must let go,
segment by segment.
I feel the gossamer
kite-string thread
slip through my hand
and I watch.

Higher and faster
she glides

        away.

To my daughter who came into my bedroom last night

and said, thank you for trusting me.
Mothers around the globe sat up
in bed and stared at the already-closed door.

The mother I was turned to gaze at me,
catching my eye in the corner mirror.
The mirrored mother knows.

She too sees the long slow hillside
in the darkened room,
the hillside I've been climbing

in Sisyphus fashion for years—
every cliché in the annals
of womanhood, parenthood, personhood.

But now, with such few words,
I find myself uncorking a daughter's refrain,
and pouring out an imagined afternoon

into my dark room, where I rest in the imagined grass,
the shadow of the imagined mountains at our backs,
and once again I see her curls, leaden with light,

and listen to her adagio hymns
as they set new seasons in motion,
relax as she toddles to an imagined corner

of an imagined garden where I can no longer
see her face, where she investigates bugs and leaves
the way she now investigates boys, girls.

And while the summer skies still spell night
and the days lie in wait, let us remain here,
with the night's cool breeze at our backs,

where she is again my stringbean daughter
and I am the gardener who never had a green thumb
but who finally learned when to stop watering.

Walking through the years—

With a light hug
and the rattle of keys,
Saturday's child
jumps into a car,
and as fast as a smile,
as fleeting as a wave,
she motors off into
a world that no
longer needs
a mother to drive.

Minister of Milk: Liam's Song

13 August 2013

Minister of Milk, Emperor of Many Hands, King of your Rectangle of Land, how you cry with constant need —such demands! Yet hear us at your gates, raising cheer, ready to trot our white flags into your castle's curtained walls. We the faithful are going nowhere. We will keep watch as you sleep in the luxury of hours, lift your coat onto your shoulders when you shiver in the dark, chant your name in the early pale of morning light. Pope of All Religion, go on—lay your weary head on our shoulders when you feel sad. We will shield you from all that's trivial—bills, meals, all that is work and all that is not. We will sing as we clean up your messes, bathe you in rosy waters, dress you in a royal wardrobe, slip slippered shoes onto your lotioned feet, take you on long walks in the cool sunshine of your perambulating throne. Tsar of a Million Spoons. Monarch of a Thousand Butterflies. Raja of Eternity's Sleepless Nights. We see the sceptre you carry and beg you to wave it across a sky of chariots. Not even 2 feet tall, mere ounces and single digit pounds, but so mighty. Cry to us, your minions. In ministerial reign, and with the courage needed for all that is yet to be seen by your beautifully cloudy eyes, a nation kneels at your *petit pois* toes, bends to kiss the very feet on which you've never stood.

Prayer

*'I dream of a world where the truth is what shapes people's politics,
rather than politics shaping what people think is true.'*
—Neil deGrasse Tyson, Astrophysicist

Sometimes I need
to not be touched
to shudder in
curl myself away from the strange noises of late
as if I am the open sore
and the breeze at the window too harsh
in its brutal touch
and I am weak and I ask for strength
    a humanity—mine, yours, ours—
armed with courage, fortitude, grit
and may we find a way to bulldoze the disorienting ways
of greed and yet I see over and over the open wounds
slashed again and again by knives of hate
hacked by swords of speech
seared by the fire of selves above selves above selves
hollowed by the bullets of today's desires
anything to make one feel more important than another
anything to make one feel he or she is worth more than another
anything to gain some kind of sick passion in a sick world
and please, I ask—can we grow trees from the mud of this life?
And still the world grows sicker
and still the wound is opening is widening is deepening
and I pray that we can find our way through this fog of hate
that maybe it really is a puff of smoke
and one can still hope it will lift
float skyward with the brightening day
and yet I fear what we will see
when morning light touches
the battlefield at dawn
I fear we will see the gaping hole of humanity
its stomach empty and hollow

so please send in the doctors
please send the human bandages
please heal this brokenhearted world
of self-serving leaders and unquestioning
followers, if not for us, for future's children
for all those we will never know
who will press on and on and on
long after we are gone—

A short, true, and not inconsequential story

Camden Town, 2016

A middle-aged woman sat on a wall as a group of teenagers in hoodies came by. It was a dark November day and the canal was cloaked in a strange shawl of thick green. The woman had been crying but she was beginning to wipe her eyes. The teenagers were talking and laughing. As they passed, one stopped. He drew back his hood and said, *It will be okay, miss. I promise.* She looked up and gave him a half smile, this boy who was half her age, and he smiled in return, kindly, as if she was his teacher, and he her favourite student. And he went on his way, back to chatting and laughing with his friends, and she went hers, lifting herself up from the wall, joining the steady throng of people moving along the city's pavements, and it seemed the evening air began to buzz with a spring-like energy in that moment. The woman found herself thinking about the many people around her and how they represented a kind of hope, faith perhaps, as they moved toward their unknown destinations, never stopping to glance her way, never pausing to see the eyes and ears and hair that belonged only to her, just as she had failed to see the eyes and ears and hair that belonged to so many others countless times before. Hundreds of people moved toward her and then moved away from her, each moving onward through their own trials and fears and struggles and heartaches and so many brutal and amazing and heartrending truths. And she became determined to speak to the strangers before her. Few would know her story but it didn't matter. Few knew her story as few know anyone's deeper stories. What matters is that the boy taught her, reminded her once again, that we write our lives in air, and that we are all strangers carrying the possible, strangers carrying love.

Weight

for Ava, April 2014

Carrying her tiny form
in the heaviness
of her sleep, her hair
still slightly damp from her bath,
her arms limp around my neck,
I lift her over
the toilet in that mundane
human activity
that is mastered with time.
And patience.
She is three.
Three years on this vast planet.
And so much on her shoulders.
How deeply unaware she is
that I have moved her at all
as I lay her back to sleep,
embedded as she is
in a dreamtime world
I cannot enter.
And this love for her?
Olympus-sized,
as heavy
as sleep itself.

Book Burning

for Michael and Elene

Bookworms of the wood-boring-beetle-kind
(not their six grown children who, when new
books arrived, devoured them one at a time)
had burrowed into their words and their rooms,
their secret storage of stories that lined
the many walls of their labyrinth home.
How fat the worms had grown with fifty silent
years of chewing, how fat and full and settled.

They set off to cull the infected books,
carefully choosing those beyond redemption,
piling them near the grinning wood fire stove
in the small nook of their coldest room. Then—
with reluctance, dismay—they fed the mouth
of the fire, stoked book by book, the pages
fanning as the grate chewed before swallowing
in one magnificent gulp—ink, spine, carbon.

They felt thinner as the fire blazed and gained
strength, until suddenly—in his hand—a lost
songbook appeared. He studied the book's changed
state and, with its heat on his knees, he flipped
its pock-marked pages and hummed a refrain.
His wife leaned near. They looked up. They nodded.
He slipped the book under his thigh, released
it from the fate of the furnace's heat.

Later, as from the pit they shovelled ashes,
the couple marvelled at how the worms ate
through their words, nibbled at long-stored memories—
the sought-after-and-found, the times-not-taken,
the what-can-never-be-lost, the times-moved-on,
and what-can-never-be-recovered, struck
most by what they found in one book's recollection—
a hymn for all they spared from time's jawing destruction.

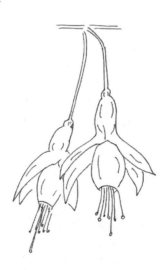

Media Luna

It was undoubtedly the feeling of exile, that sensation of a void
within which never left us, that irrational longing to hark
back to the past or else to speed up the march of time, and
those keen shafts of memory that stung like fire.
—Albert Camus, *The Plague*

Sitting in the pool, knee throbbing, I struggled
to accept this routine—my doctor's plan—
and then I saw them: an elderly couple
waiting in wheelchairs, holding hands.

A muscular man with a handsome face
kneeled at the woman's feet. She smiled at him
as he lifted her. In a square close embrace,
the woman laughed as the young man grinned.

Her bent body, wrapped in but a swimsuit,
was soon draped over his (a third her age),
as she (a third his size), allowed him to move
her down the pool's steps and onto a stage

with *caminada* paces. As they floated through
the room, this man—with a dancer's charm—
held the woman near his naked chest, then drew
her in circles, safely tucked beneath his arms.

Her cheek to his, she let him take the lead,
until, at last, she found her legs. She started
to kick, front cross, back cross, as the man ceded
his hands to hers, whispered in her ear, charting

their path. They stared into each other's eyes.
Children's calls echoed in the civic scene,
springing off hollowed walls in joyful cries.
A chlorine haze rose around them like steam.

The young man was not the only man watching
this woman's every dip, fall, sway, swoon. Casting
his eyes over water's edge, as if treading
time, a man frailer than she watched. Steadfast

observer of the counter-clockwise *caída*,
a country lost, he tried to rise from his chair
but fell back again. He quietly stared,
murmuring memories in soundless prayer—

When the last dance plays, will you clear the floor?
Return to me, Love, for one tanda more?

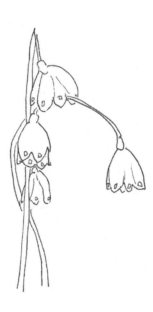

Dear Police Officer,

Please. Let me explain. No, I won't lie. Yes, I confess, I knew my time was up on that meter in the Chicago street below, where my old car sat parked, the car you were slowly circling. But I couldn't leave, you see. Sonia Sanchez was reading and Max Roach was resurrected and I was sitting between two poet-friends and, no, we weren't going anywhere as she continued to hum long after her scheduled hour was up, and you see she was telling us to move to that podium, telling us to be bold, telling us to turn and face the scorn and frowns of the men and women, the strangers and friends, who will never welcome us back, telling us to find a way to say what needs to be said, to gain the courage to *act* no matter what one's culture, colour, creed, no matter what one's gender, race, religion, no matter by what other ways and means we humans are so arbitrarily divided, and there she was calling to us, to me, to be brave, me, a woman who had hoped to learn the art of audacity by now, and time is running out, don't you see? Always running out, and sometimes we have to ignore meters running over, and she and Max began to blend as one and their rhythms began to fuse and she was moving between singing and speaking, speaking and singing, and so please forgive me, officer, as I will forgive my town, my countries, my old life and new, the history that is mine and the history that is not, and (maybe) all the so-called leaders and followers who refuse to do what needs to be done when they know, they know, they know, but I refuse to hold my tongue any longer, and forgiveness does not mean acceptance, and I'm going to stand on that pulpit, find the courage to speak loud and long, so please, officer, tell me you will see this as *case dismissed*, and that you will close your yellow notebook, tuck it back into your pocket, and shake your head a little as you walk away, crossing the street, patting the notebook, nodding a little as you say, yes, I get it. Yes, I do believe I get it.

Su Casa

You welcome me into your home
where all is so different—
the way the table is set,
the way the TV is so loud,
the way you jest,
the way your sighs are so relevant.
But I promise you this:
while I am your visitor,
I am yours.
I will eat what you eat,
drink what you drink,
and rethink what I think,
and I've even been known to speak
an accent tinged with a trace of you.
Why is this so? I've often asked myself.
Perhaps it is because you have opened
your door, greeted me
with the steam of dinner cooking,
a kiss and a smile,
that makes me
want to hang up
my coat,
pull up a chair
and listen anew
as I warm
my hands
by a fire-
side hearth
glowing
with you.

One night in September, Love

arrived,
like a swarm of bees,
as something like *vim* and
verve went everywhere
dashing, everywhere
racing, as if desperate to
cling to the rough world
—rushing—halting—buzzing—sticking—
hastening the formation of a wild new creation,
a bustling globe swollen with *affection* and
now it hangs like an ornament in
a secret slice of forest (oh, to find
what's *necessary* in this brief life) and
did you know that inside this bubble
(this hive we call home), a thousand
pockets of holy pollen soon buzzed
into being, and what choice did we
have but tuck ourselves into
the thriving evening thrum
of a million honeyed
a cappella heart-
songs
?

When the man I love asks me to dance

he says, *This is not about looks*
(not that I'd mind, to be fair)
he says, *Movies, romance, books,*
and I say no man should dare
when witnessing the crawl
of my medusa hair
or when catching the pall
of yesterday's mascara
raccooned around small,
red-veined eyes. But in the glare
of a silver-screen eclipse
this one says he swears
by my Golightly lips
my movie star figure
my Oscar winning hips
and as he praises what I fail to find
I realise he can't see otherwise,
so *hello scars, goodbye blinders,*
goodbye sheets in which we hide,
and if love is blind, I adore
its excusable delight—
for even if I rise with a roar
this one is hard to scare—
so with a *quick, close the door,*
I pull his body to my bare
hips, legs and arms tangling—
and, like that, I'm Ginger, he's Astaire,
and I'm not so good at dancing
but it's something I love to do
and I find myself romancing
this man of glowing reviews,
his play-it-again hymns,
his boy-eyed beatitudes,

and to me he is Every Man,
with his Laurence Olivier
voice, his Sidney Poitier grin—
Baby, from whence do you call?
Into the sunset we begin.
Into bed, we fall, we fall—

It doesn't spell disaster

Look at that sad case
of an *o* lying
by the side
of the road
like a flat tire
rolled from a car—
and that other *o*
half-filled as if
gasping for air
in the despair
of a too long run.
And that *v*?
See it tipped and lonely,
useless as a flipped
table. But that *ɔ*?
Perhaps it harbours
some gasping *uh*
even as it hangs
like a forgotten hook
from a ceiling.
But that blue antenna of a *y*—
it can't get any signal at all—
and that *u* has rocked to a stop—
see it leaning against
that alley wall, idly catching rain?
And that *I*—might as well
call it a boxer at the end of 10.
But the *L*, you say, is made-
of-concrete-and-wood—
a crate lift of Barthean expertise!
I watch you grip the handles,
and, like that, factory doors slide open,
and I leap up to help,

and together we march
into the ratcheting, uprighted,
spell-it-anyway-you-like noise.

Open

Seasons, you say.
All right, *shores*, I answer.
& there you go
with your *windows*,
curtains, *doors*, and me,
my *wine* & *rapport*
& you, all those
books I know
you adore.
Minds, I nod.
Hearts, you reply.
& with that
coats, *buttons*,
zippers, *hooks*
& *eyes*, *ears*, *mouths*,
& so much we *see*
& all we *overlook*
& suddenly
we are laughing,
all *toujours* this
& evermores that,
all music box *Pandora*
to the touch.

I want to die the way my dog sleeps

—a tiny, take-up-no-room-curl.
I want to live like him too
rising twice or thrice a day
a lift up from a stomach
a grin to an *n*
a head-to-tail unfurl
to a laughlined, smiling *u* face
and an *l* for a tail that (with a bolt's *click*)
triggers a merry metronomic tick
that trots my rhythm out a door
where I wander, mark,
causally claim,
a chunk of bark
and a few blades of grass
breathing *in* the glorious world
before sauntering back to that door
with a noise in my throat
a warm hand on my neck
and an *oh-wow-what-a-way-*
to-get-at-that-itchy-underskin-patch
and then—with one gulped explosion
of *my-oh-my-oh-my* and a bowl full of coolness—
the action ends
with a nonchalant stroll
back to my bed, where
I neatly collapse, twist a little
and a little more
turning and turning
and turning and turning
and, yes, turning and turning,
spiralling down and down
into the teeniest, tiniest
take-up-no-room-at-all-curl

until there is no more
Andrea: just a plain
old sleeping ball
of lower-
case
a.

Monuments of Home

The umbrella by the door
on a rainy day.
Mud-prints of a bicycle
rolled out of the way.
Cups grinning side-
ways on hooks,
tea leaves in a jar as
elegant as the crayoned portraits
taped to a fridge.
So quiet this quiet museum
I wander.
And there you are,
snug in your chair,
reading and stopping
to slumber.
I sit in a chair beside you,
open a book.
You respond
with a Saturday sigh.
A mountain range
as large and
invisible as air.
Or God.

Hannah and the garden soil

25 January 2016

No blizzard,
no missed opportunities
no drama
or early birth.
More a stirring beneath
a pattern of sun and rain,
a bright tiny thread
beaded upward
with colour and light.
And so she is.
And so she becomes.
And so a family grows
and so it succumbs
to these brave new needs
a longing for all we can
and cannot see,
our faces turning
with hers as she
adjusts her eyes
to the sun.

Transgenerational

Our brains are made up of a 100 billion nerve cells that spark and fire with astonishing speed and accuracy. And it is a source of perplexity and wonder that these neurons transmit their messages over surprising distances—sometimes up to several feet— as if throwing them around like tethered balls. But research suggests these messages might not be tethered at all, which escalates the perplexity and wonder one might feel when considering these neurons. In fact, these neurons might well catapult their messages clear across countries and seas, across generations and centuries, straight into the DNA we hold close to our hearts. And like the shrapnel of a distant war, an electric heat burns perpetually inside these neurons, and yet they are lively as children at play. Look close. You might just see the branchlike projections of dendrites reaching out to hold hands in a busy playground game, talking nonstop, excitedly shuddering the news from the past to the future and back again. Listen close. You might just hear a great conversation going on inside you—a dreamtime narrative threading into the bedsheets on which you sleep. Do not be frightened. They are there to keep you company. Put them under your pillow as dark draws near. Wrap them in your arms in the dead of a lonely night. Hear them whisper, *Do not forget. Please do not forget.*

Between my country and the others, as ministry

I cannot hear your answer, sister,
       but I know midsummer blooms. The bridge?
I'm crossing it with asters in hand—
       modest gifts of sincere exchange.
        I've come to sprig your country's paths with
        forget-me-not blues, all hues
of hyacinth tolls and gentian dues.
Please open your door. I have changed.

—after Emily Dickinson (F-40, #905)

And so everything must come to a stop

For Helen Degen Cohen, 19 November 1934 – 24 November 2015

The final page in a book we didn't want to finish.
The last song at a party we wished for all year.
The porch light snapped off as we head to bed at the end of a long day.
The trains rolling into their stations.
Letters arriving at intended destinations.
The geese flying north flying north flying north
      settling into a field near a pond,
   shaking their feathers in unison,
      sipping breaths of air as they shudder in to rest.
And you, lying in stillness
in a small hospital cube filled with the steady
beeping sound of all that slows in its effort,
and the moon outside your window hangs low in the daytime sky
telling us that things are not always as they seem.
Time is moving slower now,
which is not true at all.
It is moving the same as it always does
and yet sometimes it seems we have the power
to still the hands of clocks, press our fingers
to their fragile needles, watch the tiny spines
tremble and dissolve beneath our thumbs.
But we don't still time.
It stills us. Stills you.
Our Halinka. Witness
of history's most difficult moments
as parents were loaded onto trains
and you, small child, took the weight
of a cup in your hands and crossed
the fields alone, toward temporary safety,
and the freedom in you that followed,
in your thoughts, your beliefs, your work—work
that you so often doubted was ever to be finished,
when not-finishing was simply *you*:

the unrehearsed choreography of astonishment.
And at your hospital bedside, the promise
was made: that your words would be read
long after we—witnesses of your final breaths—
are gone, for we too will come to a stop
and every reader of these words will come to a stop,
that place of final rest, which perhaps is not rest at all,
more a stepping out of a body to let others pass,
a slowing into that final station, where one reaches
a hand through a carriage window to unlatch a door,
steps onto the platform of this floating vessel
called time, and now you—here, that urgent look
in your eyes, that mischievous smile on your face,
waving at me through the mist that rises
between what is *now* and what was *then*,
and from your open hand sheets of paper
catch in the wind and I run to them, pulling them
close as you make your way over the tracks
to a sister who waits at the edge of a field,
still and cool and bright—

The Wildflowers of La Hille

'we shall laugh, and institutions will curl up like burnt paper'
DH Lawrence, 'Escape'

—for Cas

What is held in the air of La Hille?
Wildflowers nod as if they know.
Wildflowers nod as if to say,
It is what the wind releases,
it is what the sky sees,
it is all that is held in
stories of seed, tales of soil,
sun's love and rain's need.
For what is time, my darlings,
but a string of notes swept
along life's vineyard paths?
Dreams linger still,
here, where conversations
seep into colours of petal
and stem, sepal and style,
where green stems rehearse
earth's chorus of delight.
And surely this too is
what it means to be human,
what it means to be possible,
what it means when one
gives another the sun to hold.
Faces turn upward toward the sky.
In the faces: seeds. In the seeds: us.
We wake in the flowers of La Hille
where colour smiles up at the sun—
where unlying life is an oceanwide field
and we dive into all we become.

That which once was

A rocking foam of memory nods to me
like the goodbye of a thousand waving hands.

Dear child, what unconscious tune
do you hum as you splash, pour, swim away?

Tell me: how is it that you are *this*
even when you've long left *this* behind

like the cowry shell forgotten on your windowsill,
years after you've shaken loose a mother's need?

So much remains swaddled in our *never-mores*,
like this one that clings to sky's evening light

the slow burn that pulls the departed behind
like the bright turning of *away, ever, beyond.*

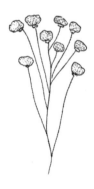

Qumran

for Peter

Scrolled parchment, spiralled into safe-
keeping. Texts pressed, snailed into cells.

Flesh scrolled into mine, just an arm
spun over my waist, my back pressed

to a stomach, hips spooled into parchment
of thighs, hands domed beneath fingers

intersticed, fingers that shudder every so often,
as if to remind me that morning is not yet,

as if to say 4am is but a bookmark,
an airlocked reserve, a reed pen,

a cave of punctuation mark. *Aide-
mémoire.* Where-to-return. Papyrus

of iron-gall and carbon soot sheets,
we are tucked into as little space as possible,

in these coils of elsewhere. Nobody knows
us here and we can hardly decipher it ourselves,

yet if this dead sea life is but an afterthought
of words without words, sleep without sleep,

then leave me here, pressed between
mornings, coppered into clay pot dark.

Time zones and the art of healing

I

The last thing to be caught
is air, the way it parts for us,
      our invisible blood-red sea,
holding days open like curtains
      on a windowsill stage,
      framing the glassed impediments of agony,
      even as we move onward, forward,
      in steel ages of flight, the wind
stealing the sealed gifts
      of minutes that bubble up
just beyond our grasp,
          as we move west,
          as we move,
          as we—

II

How does the sky
   unfurl hours not before known?
What do we erase in the circular awl,
   corkscrewing round and down,
     where so much is contained,
        invisible, outlying still?

III

Once, for a whole year, I thought
I was older than I was. I couldn't
be bothered to do the math.
When my husband pointed out
my blunder, I felt as if I had entered
the daylight savings of life,
winning back the year I had lost.

IV

Forgetting of all kinds bores
into the fleshy sides of time,
    pockmarking memory
            as it runs ahead like
    a child at the beach,
        carving a path along
                the cliff-edge of water,
    a child who looks back smiling,
            dangerously near sea's verge,
                    and no matter how fast we move,
    she is faster still, her hair coppered
            in the sun, her laugh always—

V

We too are the plane-wing awl
cutting into wood-fired clouds
where the sun refuses to set—
a light racing onward—
and we will never know
what it means for the body
to stand still until
it is too late to do
anything but—
and I miss you
and all that floats just ahead
in air and clouds
beckoning me with absent hands
and a so-long smile
and the shadow cast on the
tiny towns and roads
and cars that move
like toys below—

VI

Wait long enough, move long enough,
    and maybe we'll find the crossroads, midsky—
        there, where the west again becomes east,
    where east again becomes west,
        where curtains relax, windows open,
            and in the gust that enters like a gasp,
time and motion
        will slip away,
    all pain becomes absorbed,
            silent,
        all life,
                    all death,
                        directionless—

Bookends

—Goodbye
frames our lives
like two warm palms
supporting the upright
spines of our fierce,
fierce love. We live on hellos,
the slippage of savoury words
from the shelves, cherishing
the pages turning in our mouths,
even as we must, ever over,
swallow our tears, shut the covers,
slip our souls back into place
and once again whisper,
Goodbye, darling.
                    Goodbye—

Notes

'Between my Country and the Others, a Sea' and 'Between my Country and the Others—as Ministry': F-40 refers to Facsimile 40, the last of Emily Dickinson's archived hand-made manuscripts.

'The Slug': *casarecce* is a Sicilian pasta that resembles small rolled-up scrolls. The word literally means 'homemade'.

'Blood Ties, circa 1932': an achene (used as adjective here) is a dry fruit in which a single seed is encased in a shell or husk (such as a dandelion seed).

'*Gemütlichkeit*': there is no English equivalent for this German word, but perhaps it's best described as a deep sense of peace of mind and shared feelings of comfort, warmth, acceptance and belonging.

'Forgetting this problem of dirt and dust': calyces is the plural of calyx, referring to both the base of a flower (that holds everything together) and to any cuplike cavity such as the chambers of the kidney.

'Proprioception': the body's ability to orientate itself in space in regards to inside and outside sensory cues.

'Root Position': *agrément* is a French musical notation for embellishment; a fermata is the musical notation that allows a note or chord to be held for as long as desired; and the pinblock is the unseen heart of a piano on which tuning pins are anchored and held taut to create pitch.

'Media Luna': in the Argentine tango, *caminada* incorporates walking movements in which the steps are upright and in a narrow track, while a *caída* is a position in which the principal dancer steps backwards on a supporting leg while the partner steps forward on a supporting leg so that the two are standing as one.

'Dear Police Officer,': Sonia Sanchez is a poet, playwright, professor, activist and was a major influence in the Black Arts and Civil Rights

Movements of the 1960s. Max Roach was a jazz drummer and composed many works used in plays, films and dance pieces. During this evocative and powerful reading at Harold Washington Library in Chicago, Sanchez sang some of her poetry with a percussion-type beat inspired by Roach.

'When the man I love asks me to dance': Golightly refers to the Audrey Hepburn character in *Breakfast at Tiffany's*.

'It doesn't spell disaster': Barthean refers to Roland Barthes, who believed the only time humans are released from the ideology and biases embedded in the very language we speak is when we are, even if briefly, deeply (ecstatically) in love.

'Qumran': the archaeological site of caves in the West Bank where the Dead Sea Scrolls were found.

'Transgenerational': transgenerational trauma refers to trauma that passes through generations. Not only can someone experience trauma, theories suggest, but they can then pass the symptoms and behaviours of trauma survival on to their children, who then might further pass these along the family line. Dendrites are projections of neurons (nerve cells) that receive information from other neurons through chemical signals and electric impulses.

Acknowledgements

No book is an island. More they are invisible countries populated by vast numbers of invisible people, and I am incredibly grateful to so many who helped make this book possible.

Heartfelt thanks goes to the editors of the following journals and anthologies for their encouragement and support by first publishing some of the poems in this collection (sometimes in earlier renditions):

Acumen: 'Standing near my father's work' and 'Bookends'; *All We Can Hold: A Collection of Poetry on Motherhood* (Sage Hill Press): 'To my daughter who came into my bedroom last night' and 'What recovery looks like'; *The Adirondack Review*: 'The Psychologists' Room'; *Ambit*: 'Between my country and the others, as ministry'; *Bared: an anthology* (Les Femmes Folles Books): 'Just another breast poem'; *Bellevue Literary Review*: 'Inscripted'; *Compass Magazine*: 'The Time-being of Oak' and 'The Daffodils'; *Crab Orchard Review*: 'The Incubator'; *Ginosko Literary Journal*: 'Appellations' and 'Self-Portrait, Desk'; *The Inflectionist Review*: 'Disguises' and 'Time Zones and the Art of Healing' (nominated for a Pushcart); *Jet Fuel Review*: 'Root Position'; *Lascaux Review*: 'At a Truck Stop on Highway 124' (nominated for a Pushcart); *London Grip*: 'Monuments of Home'; *Lunch Ticket*: 'It doesn't spell disaster' and 'I want to die the way my dog sleeps'; *Kettle Blue Review*: 'Minister of Milk: Liam's Song'; *Meridian*: 'Lymphatic' (runner up in Meridian's Flash Fiction Prize); *Mid-American Review*: 'Panoply' (finalist in the MAR's FineLine Prize); *Nimrod International Journal of Prose and Poetry*: 'Geometric'; *Mezzo Cammin*: 'Book Burning' and 'Spindles, Time, Cancer'; *Pacific Review*: 'The New Bed'; *Poetry East*: 'Llama: lama glama'; *Pirene's Fountain*: 'Between my country and the others, a sea' and 'That which once was'; *Rappahannock Review*: 'The Palm of Proprioception' and 'Last Day to Save on Sarah Jaeger's "Throwing and Alternative Video"'; *Red Sky: poetry on the global epidemic of violence against women* (Sable Books): 'Dear Police Officer,'; *Segue Online Literary Journal*: 'Regret'; *Spoon River Poetry Review*: 'Blood Ties, circa 1932'; *Tupelo Quarterly*: 'The Unreliable Patient,' 'Qumran,' and 'Ode to the

Stairs,' (respectively runner-up, semi-finalist, and finalist in TQ open contests); *Under the Radar*: 'Open'; *Written River: A Journal of Eco-Poetics*: 'Lessons from the Queen of the Lasius Niger'

Huge amounts of gratitude and love also goes out to the Poetry Exchange beauties (you know who you are) who created new kinds of space, literal and otherwise, to grow my writing, my art and my own kind of flowers; my Southbank writing group who inspire me constantly; Jamie McGarry and the Valley Press team who gave this book the best kind of home, including Jo Brandon whose editorial skills are second to none, and Peter Barnfather, whose incredible design skills made this book what it is; various friends and poets, some alive, some no longer, who continue to remind me through their talent and hard work to be steadfast and humble; my family on both sides of the Atlantic, including and especially Ava, Liam and Hannah; Nicole and Elizabeth; Chessie, P and Oli; and Peter, who never fails to understand, love and believe in me and in this strange work called poetry.

These poems also carry the loving memory
of two brothers who celebrated this book with me
long before it was published.

Peter Maurice Joseph Slot, 3 December 1932 – 15 October 2020
and
Michael Maurice Gerald Philip Slot, 24 October 1929 – 2 January 2018

You are missed by many.

*You cannot do a kindness too soon, for you
never know how soon it will be too late.*

—Ralph Waldo Emerson